PRACTICAL SPIRITUAL WARFARE

The Devil didn't make me do it.

Mike Dillard

ISBN-13: 9798646591242

Cover design by: Art Painter
Library of Congress Control Number: 2018675309
Printed in the United States of America

First and foremost, I would like to dedicate this book to the Lord Jesus Christ and to His Church. His Church has been not only my mission but also my teacher in many ways. Thank God for His Holy Spirit, that He has promised would lead us into all truth. I remain a learner in His school of life.

Secondly, I want to acknowledge my wife of over 50 years. Pauline continues to be soul-mate, friend, confidant, encourager, and my love. When I have doubted, she has lifted me. When I needed encouragement, she has always been in my corner. She surely is a gift from the Lord's hand to me. To our four children she has been not only a mother, but a constant supporter, full of grace and God's love.

To countless others that have impacted my life, too many to enumerate, I give a special thanks. You have challenged me not only in my walk, but your hungry hearts have propelled me to push farther in to the wondrous beauty that the Lord has for His Bride. Together, in His time, we will join Him.

Special thanks to my daughter in-law, Elizabeth Dillard, and her artistry. Her simple handmade greeting cards, Luna Noodle Art, have always been just right for the occasion. She was the first one I thought of to help me with the book cover. Nice job and thanks Liz.

CONTENTS

GETTING STARTED

In order to really understand Spiritual Warfare we must start at the beginning. This is vital, for it gives us the foundation that is necessary to grasp the inward and outward battles that we face as Christians.

The God-head in conference declares, "Let Us make man in Our image, according to Our likeness; and let them rule over the fish of the sea and over the birds of the sky and over the cattle and over all the earth, and over every creeping thing that creeps on the earth." (Gen 1:26) This man, made in the image of God, was given authority of all before him.

War had already been declared by one who had fallen from heaven. He traveled under various aliases, Satan, Beelzebub, Father of Lies, Accuser, Abaddon, Devil, this evil one, once called Lucifer (light-bearer), was the first to rebel against God. He was summarily thrown out of heaven and cast down to the earth, where he became known as the "prince of the power of the air".[1] [2] The lines in the sand had been drawn. The good guys and the bad guys have arrayed themselves in battle. Their forces are hidden from the natural eye, but they are nonetheless real. The prize for the conqueror is the world and all of humanity. The stage was set for this battle of the ages many years ago in, of all places, a garden. The serpent would wait for just the right moment to sow doubt and to challenge man to choose his own path, instead of the ways of God.

As usual, it started out very simply, just avoid one tree, that's it nothing else, just don't eat from that tree. Adam didn't try to negotiate an exception. He made the choice to do what he wanted to do. Sound familiar. "Hey, we eat everything else; why not eat some of this tree as well? We know God really loves us; why would He deny us something we really want. Maybe if we don't eat the whole thing and split it between the two of us it would be all right."

Doesn't seem like much but that one taste of forbidden fruit plunged man irrevocably into all out warfare against powers and principalities and creation itself. Death would reign throughout the world. Its impact would touch all of the natural fauna and flora, and every man woman and child that would ever be born.

Doesn't seem fair does it? Why would a loving God allow one man's rebellion to impact the lives and eternal destinies of untold millions?

The answer is relatively simple to those of us that are not biblical scholars and yet remains eternally profound. God created a man and a woman, breathed life into them and enabled them to reproduce genetically others who would be physically and spiritually like themselves. Instead of robotic obedience, God also gave man the rich gift of "choice". The problem with having the gift of "choice" is, choices have consequences. Their descendants as a result of that initial act of rebellion would carry within themselves the seeds of rebellion and death. The spirit part of all mankind became dead and separated from God, the source of life. The difficulty was, God allowed them to choose.

Let us not forget the, not insignificant, role the old serpent played in the scheme of things. When God created man He made him the ruler over all creatures great and small. The earth was to be His domain.[3] At one point Adam even had the rule over that old slithering serpent. That is the reason Satan was so crafty in approaching the weak link of the team of Adam and Eve. Adam had personally been told by God "Don't eat of that tree."[4] Evidently he did not communicate to Eve the same import of the command, he had received. Adam had been given dominion/rule over all that crept on the ground and he did not exercise his authority to properly inform Eve nor to deal with the serpent. In choosing not to walk in the authority the Lord had given him, he inadvertently gave his authority to his adversary; from this point forward the spirit of man would be dead with reference to God. Score one for Satan and his minions.[5] [6]

(In heeding the suggestion/temptation of Satan, Adam was choosing someone other than God as his source. At its root, his choice was not believing what God had said and accepting the word of Satan as truth, thus rebellion against God.)

This separation from God which became the legacy of all men is simply called sin. This "sin principle" is resident in everyone regardless of having committed any transgression whether in thought or deed. Any action, motive, or desire, expressed or hidden in the inner man which is generated from the indwelling "sin principle" is also referred to as a sin. Therefore, sin resides in every man. The result is we are not only "sinners" by inheritance but we "sin", which is the outworking and reflection of our inherited nature. I guess apples don't fall far from the tree, we came by our failings honestly, for Adam was our great, great, etc. grandfather.

Without re-writing Biblical history, let us jump to the Jewish nation. God in His wisdom chose one group of people to which He would reveal His nature and His laws. His desire was to show that His nature and His laws were in actuality beyond their attainment and they could never fully meet the demands of His righteous nature or His laws. Instead of hearing the heart of God behind all the laws, they made their own traditions and religious ceremonies a mere hiding place for the darkness of their hearts. Ceremony took the place of relationship; in essence they "missed the point". As in the beginning, God was looking for people who would choose to walk with Him in close fellowship, without all the trappings of ritual and formality. I can hear the words of Jesus,

"You have heard ..., but I say to you "[7]

Jesus came into the world to not only be our Savior but to introduce us to the Father. Everything that Jesus did and said was a direct response to the Father by the Holy Spirit. He was the exact representation of the Godhead.[8] He said in reference to Himself, "He who has seen Me has seen the Father."[9] He even taught us to pray, "Our Father who is in heaven,..."[10] Also, "In that day you will not question Me about anything. Truly, truly, I say to you, if you ask the Father for anything in My name, He will give it to you."[11]

Because of our myopic vision, we have tended to look at the substitutional work of Christ and our derived benefit, forgiveness of sin and eternal life as God's eventual goal. As a result we rally around John 3:16[12], and rightly rejoice at the wondrous gift of salvation. Yet, in reality we are still missing the point, though we receive this incredible gift of grace, it still is not all about us. Even the gift of redemption is only a part of God's divine plan, for He dealt with us, as with Israel, for His names sake.[13] [14] We definitely receive the benefits, but His consummate plan is greater than we have thought. (Also check out Ephesians chapter 1)

In brief, what was God's purpose, His goal, from the beginning of creation, including the formation of man? In Genesis we see God walking with Adam and in my mind's eye I see them walking and talking as friends, maybe Adam was getting further instructions on how to keep the garden with which he had been entrusted. During some of those times of fellowship, I can hear Adam being thankful for all of his surroundings and for the incredible creatures that populated his slice of God's creation. We may never know exactly what was said, at least not in this life. But it is obvious that it was God's desire to have a close relationship with these two humans that would become the grandparents of every nation and tongue on the earth.

WELCOME TO SPIRITUAL WARFARE

His desire from the "get go" was to have a people, a family that would choose Him as their source and provider. A family of individuals in "His image and likeness"[15], that desire was thwarted by the choices made by Adam and Eve in the garden. Thwarted but not forgotten by God just delayed as He worked to bring about what the Scriptures call "the fullness of time". It was at that opportune time; Christ took upon Himself flesh and became "God incarnate"[16]. He was to be the "First born among many brethren"[17], the family the Father had desired. His sacrificial example and His teachings were to exemplify and reflect the Father's goal of having a Family, "in His image".

The utter impossibility of humans, in our own strength and will power, to achieve the Lord's goal, was met with God's provision. He sent His Spirit to dwell in us. Believers became the Holy Spirit's habitation, His house, His temple, His dwelling place. The Holy Spirit was to become the enabling force of change, by His conviction and graceful provision; He would bring about a people after God's own heart, a people in the likeness of God.

Multiplied millions have come out of darkness and into the marvelous light of the Lord Jesus Christ through the centuries. The Church has not only grown numerically but since the Apostolic age there has also been a continuing restoration of truth that was for the most part forgotten during the "Dark Ages" of religious bigotry and error. This restoration continues in these days in which we are now living, irreversibly moving to the culmination of God's desire.

At this point we are able to see that God the Father is preparing for Himself a family and this family was to be made "in His image". The Holy Spirit was constructing the temple/house in which He would dwell and manifest the grace and supply that only God could give, exemplifying the "Christ life". But, what about Jesus, in the plan of God, was there something unique that awaited Him? Absolutely, He awaited His bride?

In order to answer that question more fully let us look at a principle found in the book of Genesis chapter two, it is best seen as God brings the animals to Adam to be named. The Lord knew that it wasn't good for Adam to be alone[18] so out of His creation He brought animals and birds, to Adam and whatever he called them that became their name. It must have been a busy day, not to mention a demonstration of Adam's intellectual ability in identifying all of God's creatures.[19]

God probably brought the animals and birds to Adam in pairs and it didn't take Adam long to realize there was none that were suitable for him. God already knew that, but wanted Adam to realize it for himself. Notice, only after bringing all the animals before Adam to be named, was it time for God to put Adam to sleep in order to create his perfect mate, one fit especially for Adam.

How do you come up with one that would be suitable for Adam? Only one way, the one suitable for Adam must come out of Adam. God removed a rib and fashioned his bride, Eve. Adam's basic response, paraphrased, was "Wow! For me?" He had found his suitable helpmate, one who was like him.

I point to this principle because it hasn't changed, in order for the Lord Jesus Christ to have a bride; she must have the same divine life and character that flowed through His being. As Eve was taken out of Adam, the bride must receive her life and likeness from the Son. His bride must be like Him, suitable for the Son of God. Not divided, immature and world oriented, but one like Himself.[20]

The stature of the bride is best articulated in the book of Ephesians. Ephesians 1:22, 23 "And He put all things in subjection under His feet, and gave Him as head over all things to the church, which is His body, the fullness of Him who fills all in all." His body was to be the fullest expression of His person.
Also in Ephesians 4: 13" ... until we all attain to the unity of the faith, and of the knowledge of the Son of God, to a mature man, to the measure of the stature which belongs to the fullness of Christ." The stature of the bride was to perfectly complement the Son of God. A bride fit for the King, not lacking in beauty, fully fit for the Bridegroom. She, because of the inner workings of the Holy Spirit, will faithfully reflect the image of the Son of God.

In order to receive this glorious bride for Himself, He set to work to accomplish the seeming impossible. The Lord Jesus would assume the responsibility and work with us and in us to bring about His desire. Read Ephesians 5:25-27. "Just as Christ also loved the church and gave Himself up for her, so that He might sanctify her, having cleansed her by the washing of water with the word (Gk. rhema), that He might present to Himself the church in all her glory, having no spot or wrinkle or any such thing; but that she would be holy and blameless."

God's purpose from creation is to be fulfilled in the Church. Not the Church that we currently see but a transformed body of believers. There is a Church it seems, within the church that we see around us, being formed in His likeness. The status quo will not cut it. Church as usual will not cut it. There is a fight going on. It is a fight to the finish. Only those who overcome will receive a new name and a crown of life.[21]

Most when they read the title "Practical Spiritual Warfare" instantly think of dealing with demonic forces and the subtleties of temptation the enemy throws at us. Indeed that is a part of this warfare, but it is not the predominant portion. As we continue I think it will be obvious the major offensive which must be dealt with is within the heart of man. By the end of our study, we will be able to throw out the excuse, "the devil made me do it" and take charge of our own lives with a new sense of authority and destiny.

Later we will deal with the issue of deliverance from demonic forces and entities. This will be handled in its proper context. A wise man once said, "You cannot cast out the carnal nature." It would be nice, but it is just not going to happen.

Our old man is dealt with at the cross of Christ. We can readily see this in the following Scriptures.

Rom 6: 1-7 What shall we say then? Are we to continue in sin so that grace may increase? May it never be! How shall we who died to sin still live in it? Or do you not know that all of us who have been baptized into Christ Jesus have been baptized into His death? Therefore we have been buried with Him through baptism into death, so that as Christ was raised from the dead through the glory of the Father, so we too might walk in newness of life. For if we have become united with *Him* in the likeness of His death, certainly we shall also be *in the likeness* of His resurrection, knowing this, that our old self was crucified with *Him,* in order that our body of sin might be done away with, so that we would no longer be slaves to sin; for he who has died is freed from sin.

GOD DESIRES FRUIT

It seems that the Lord has a special place in His heart for gardens and farming. His first dealings with man was in a garden He had planted. Genesis 2:8 "The LORD God planted a garden toward the east, in Eden; and there He placed the man whom He had formed." In a sense God sublet the garden and the earth to Adam with certain terms, as is the right of any owner. The stipulations were made plain, rule over what I have given you, be fruitful and multiply, and don't eat from the tree of the knowledge of good and evil.[22]

Nothing was withheld from Adam; truly Eden was a beautiful place. It was a veritable sensory feast, beautiful blossoming trees, and aromatic flowers growing around. To eat was nothing more than reaching up and plucking tantalizing fruit from the trees or gathering a handful of berries or grapes from the various vines and shrubs. One could eat until he was completely satisfied.

Animals cavorted around them without fear. Birds sang their wondrous musical praise to Almighty God. Eagles soared high above as if pointing to the Creator and rejoicing in the freedom of flight. All was in order, nothing was amiss. Adam walked and talked with God openly without a sense of self-consciousness, fear or condemnation.[23]

Then, darkness fell; death came on the scene for the first time. Man became spiritually dead to God. His consciousness of self became ignited; the beginnings of the all important "I". All creation came under the same sentence of separation and loss, nothing was spared. The judgment of the "Land Owner" was swift and entirely within His rights. "You are free; just don't eat from that tree." By Adam's single rebellious transgression all men were made sinners.[24]

The creation of God was temporarily marred and could not produce the expected fruit. Men would no longer reproduce those who would bear the "image of God". Their very nature was fallen, no longer in communion, no longer reflecting His glorious person. And creation itself became subject to futility and death.[25]

It wasn't until the time of Christ, that God could once again expect fruitfulness. The created world would still be under the curse of death and separation. Man would still be set apart from God by his inward sin nature. But, God's provision arrived in the person of the Lord Jesus Christ. To those that would trust in Him and choose to affirm their reception of the new order of things, the New Covenant. They would become the people who could produce the kind of fruit that God was looking for. A people who walked in obedience to the two greatest commandments, they would love God and love their neighbor.[26]

At last, God could begin to see godly fruit in a people that would bear the name Christian. It wasn't an overnight work, but it was a start. Through the Spirits discipline and God's sovereign use of circumstances He would transform those to whom He had granted believing faith[27] to move from barrenness to fruitfulness.

We see this best exemplified in the book of John chapter 15 verses 1-8. "I am the true vine, and My Father is the vinedresser. Every branch in Me that does not bear fruit, He takes away; and every *branch* that bears fruit, He prunes it so that it may bear more fruit. You are already clean because of the word which I have spoken to you. Abide in Me, and I in you. As the branch cannot bear fruit of itself unless it abides in the vine, so neither *can* you unless you abide in Me. I am the vine, you are the branches;

he who abides in Me and I in him, he bears much fruit, for apart from Me you can do nothing. If anyone does not abide in Me, he is thrown away as a branch and dries up; and they gather them, and cast them into the fire and they are burned. If you abide in Me, and My words abide in you, ask whatever you wish, and it will be done for you. My Father is glorified by this, that you bear much fruit, and *so* prove to be My disciples."

Jesus in these verses speaks of the Father as the "vinedresser", the one who oversees the vineyard. Our Father, the Gardener, the Land Owner, once again takes His place as the Overseer Who cultivates His estate. Notice that in Eden the cultivation was the responsibility was Adams, that didn't work out so well. Now, God Himself assumes the responsibility of pruning His human garden. Nothing is left to chance. Our only job is to respond and yield to His discipline as His child.[28]

This "abiding" lifestyle, spoken of by Jesus, was the restoration of a broken relationship due to the fall in Eden. Hearts that had been seared and dead with reference to God had come alive by the indwelling Spirit of Christ.[29] Communication lines were restored. God was no longer far off, but as close as your next breath. 1 John 3:2 "Beloved, now we are children of God, and it has not appeared as yet what we will be. We know that when He appears, we will be like Him, because we will see Him just as He is."

Please note the last portion of verse 2 quoted above, "we will be like Him". Can you grasp the Lord's desire? From Genesis to Revelation He has purposed to have those who would bear His likeness. Left to our own devices, we were without hope. God dealt with the issue of the sin nature by the death of Christ. And He dealt with the problem of our failures, faults, our sins, by the same power which raised Jesus from the dead, the indwelling Spirit of Christ.[30]

Because of the weakness of the human condition and their marked inability to produce the kind of fruit God was looking for and in keeping with His desire to express His life in and through men, God became the ultimate equipper. To those who would turn to Christ as Lord, He would give His Spirit. As individuals yielded to His presence within, they would manifest the fruit of Christ thus expressing His nature.[31]

Galatians 5: 22-23 But the fruit of the Spirit is love, joy, peace, patience, kindness, goodness, faithfulness, gentleness, self-control; against such things there is no law. These verses in Galatians exemplify the fruit the Father is after in those who are abiding in Christ. The beauty of His expectation is we are not left alone to fend for ourselves against the many battles within and without. Thank God for the answer also found in Galatians 5: 16-18. "But I say, walk by the Spirit, and you will not carry out the desire of the flesh. For the flesh sets its desire against the Spirit, and the Spirit against the flesh; for these are in opposition to one another, so that you may not do the things that you please. But if you are led by the Spirit, you are not under the Law. Also in Galatians 5:25 we read "If we live by the Spirit, let us also walk by the Spirit."

OUR HEART, OUR GARDEN

Matthew 13:3-9 And He spoke many things to them in parables, saying, "Behold, the sower went out to sow; and as he sowed, some *seeds* fell beside the road, and the birds came and ate them up. Others fell on the rocky places, where they did not have much soil; and immediately they sprang up, because they had no depth of soil. But when the sun had risen, they were scorched; and because they had no root, they withered away. Others fell among the thorns, and the thorns came up and choked them out. And others fell on the good soil and *yielded a crop, some a hundred-fold, some sixty, and some thirty. He who has ears, let him hear."

It seems it is always easier to ascribe the application of certain scriptures to someone other than ourselves. Surely, once we have turned to Christ as Lord the above verses no longer apply to us, because we must already be the "good soil".

Let's get brutally honest with each other. Is all the soil of your heart "good soil"? Are you holding anything back? In those dark recesses is there dried up rocky places? To be truthful, we all have areas that we are not proud of. Places that need to be brought to the light, and sometimes it's not even a "bad" thing it's just something we feel we should not be doing or thinking. Now is the time to hoe out the weeds; maybe plow that area with prayer and confession.[32]

There is a promise in the book of Exodus God gave to His people before they entered Canaan. Their enemies were mighty and numerous but if they would obey His voice, He would be an enemy to their enemies.[33] In the same chapter He also says and I quote, "I will not drive them out before you in a single year, that the land may not become desolate and the beasts of the field become too numerous for you. I will drive them out before you little by little, until you become fruitful and take possession of the land."[34] God wanted to be sure they could handle all the land which would become their possession.

In our day, our first response to that statement might be, "Father, please get rid of all my problems and destroy all my enemies right now. Don't leave one thing that can hinder my walk with You." Our Heavenly Father is much wiser than that, His desire is for us to face our problems and enemies head on. Then by listening to His voice and heeding His guidance we "little by little" learn to make our "heart garden" pleasing to our King.[35] It is only those things we have purchased with the pain and joy of triumph that really belong to us. It is in that place we find true "ownership" of the ground beneath our feet.

Have you ever noticed, especially as a young Christian, when you first learn a Scriptural premise, you actually believe the benefit you have learned is yours and you are ready for battle in that area? It is only later when you are faced with an insurmountable mountain and your heart fails and faith wavers that you call upon the Lord and He answers. You may need to fight, stand against unbelief, and draw on the Lord's resources, but eventually you come out victorious. Now you no longer have just the knowledge of something, but by experience you now own the reality of the promise. Knowledge puffs up, but Spirit given revelation through experience generates ownership of God's provisions. With ownership there comes future victories and the ability to overcome in this and in other battlegrounds we may face.

As stated earlier, God will not leave the cultivation of His human garden entirely up to us. It is ours to yield, trust and obey the Comforter that now lives within us. So, how are we to cooperate with the Holy Spirit to see the transformation of our inner man, to be one who bears the image of God?

First things first, we must acknowledge that we are unable to eradicate the "sin nature" we inherited from Adam. Secondly, we need to admit our inability to bring our fleshly and worldly desires completely under control without help. Both of these responses require true humility. This should not be a problem if we come into agreement with God's perspective found in 1 Corinthians. "For consider your calling, brethren, that there were not many wise according to the flesh, not many mighty, not many noble; but God has chosen the foolish things of the world to shame the wise, and God has chosen the weak things of the world to shame the things which are strong, and the base things of the world and the despised God has chosen, the things that are not, so that He may nullify the things that are, so that no man may boast before God."[36]

THE OLD MAN IS DEAD

I have prayed for many years for those in the Church to finally admit they are weak and that aside from the intervention of Christ and the strength he gives, we can do absolutely nothing. Most would nod in agreement with this statement, but it is one thing to say it, it is another thing to live it. Even Paul the apostle would acknowledge his dependence on Christ. "I can do all things through Him who strengthens me." And, "I have been crucified with Christ; and it is no longer I who live, but Christ lives in me; and the *life* which I now live in the flesh I live by faith in the Son of God, who loved me and gave Himself up for me."[37]

There is an irrefutable fact in Scriptures that is seldom talked about and rarely understood by the majority of believers. It is found in Romans chapters 6, 7, and 8. The old nature which was of Adam's seed becomes dead when one accepts Christ as Savior. This is a fact, not a theory. It is a done deal, no exceptions. "Or do you not know that all of us who have been baptized into Christ Jesus have been baptized into His death? Therefore we have been buried with Him through baptism into death, so that as Christ was raised from the dead through the glory of the Father, so we too might walk in newness of life. For if we have become united with *Him* in the likeness of His death, certainly we shall also be *in the likeness* of His resurrection, knowing this, that our old self was crucified with *Him,* in order that our body of sin might be done away with, so that we would no longer be slaves to sin; for he who has died is freed from sin."[38]

Let's see if we can't break these verses down just a little for people like me who have read them many times but didn't quite grasp what was being said. If I tend to oversimplify forgive me, it's the only way I can really get a handle on the writings of Paul.[39]

We were baptized into the body of Christ by the Spirit of God.[40] This occurred when we first accepted Him as our Savior of which water baptism was our open statement of having received Christ as Lord. By a sovereign act of God, what was dead in relation to God, our "old man" was deemed by God to have been crucified with Christ. This old "Adam nature" by a divine intervention was killed. Please understand this, the link to Adam's lineage was broken; we need not be dominated or ruled by what God had delivered us from. This took care of the indwelling "sin nature" and separation from God. Now we have the opportunity to walk before God in the "newness of Life".[41]

The part in us which propelled us and motivated us to commit sins was "done away with". Whereas before it seemed we were driven by an inward force to obey our ungodly desires. We now have the privilege and freedom of choice for the first time. With our choices we would also be responsible for the consequences of our choices. Understand, prior to accepting the Lord you could make choices as well but regardless of the decisions made, good or bad, you remained far from God. The "sin nature" was a constant barrier.

At this point, we now have charge of our "garden". A wise man once told me, "What you feed grows, what you starve dies." In the language of gardening, "What you plant and cultivate grows, what you weed out dies." The question becomes what are you feeding and what are you cultivating in the garden of your heart?

Now as never before you are completely responsible for your own spiritual growth. Only you can determine the depth of your relationship with Christ, not your pastor or elder, not your friends or family, not even the culture you are living in. It's your choice. Your "old man" is dead and the power of a new life resides in you, all you need, is to obey and be led by the Holy Spirit.[42]

Christians who take the responsibility of their walk seriously step up their effort to avoid temptation and labor diligently to not sin. They incessantly strive to keep sin in abeyance. While it is true we must strive to keep ourselves in right relationship with the Lord, the question becomes, what is the source of our striving? It can't be by obeying laws, for we all know that the law brings death not life.[43] Maybe in the strength of our will we can force our body and soul to conform to God's plan. This, though the desire is commendable, brings us back to choosing ourselves as the source of life and not God.

The answer lies in the Scripture found in Romans eight verses 12 and 13, "So then, brethren, we are under obligation, not to the flesh, to live according to the flesh for if you are living according to the flesh, you must die; but if by the Spirit you are putting to death the deeds of the body, you will live." It seems many of us are driven by the fear of falling. This fear is manifested much like one trying to walk on a tightrope. The harder one tries not to fall, the more surely they suffer the consequences of gravity. Try this, when faced with the tightrope, relax, don't panic, you are not alone. You have been here before and you know already how many times you have tried and failed, so admit it to the Lord. "Lord, my way is not working. I need Your help." This is what He was after anyhow, for you to realize your dependence upon Him. YOU CAN MAKE IT!!!

1 John 4:4b "...because greater is He who is in you than he who is in the world."

Philippians 4:13 "I can do all things through Him who strengthens me."

CHOICES

OK, my "old man" is dead, why do I still sin? Choices, we sin when we choose to go our own way, regardless of the inner promptings of the Holy Spirit. In the words of James, "Let no one say when he is tempted, "I am being tempted by God"; for God cannot be tempted by evil, and He Himself does not tempt anyone. But each one is tempted when he is carried away and enticed by his own lust. Then when lust has conceived, it gives birth to sin; and when sin is accomplished, it brings forth death."[44] Someone wiser than myself once said, "You can't stop the birds from flying around your head, but you can definitely keep them from building a nest."

The question arises, what is your life style relative to your walk with God? Let's look at 1 John chapter 3 verses 7 through 9, "Little children, make sure no one deceives you; the one who practices righteousness is righteous, just as He is righteous; the one who practices sin is of the devil; for the devil has sinned from the beginning. The Son of God appeared for this purpose, to destroy the works of the devil. No one who is born of God practices sin, because His seed abides in him; and he cannot sin, because he is born of God."

I believe the Amplified Bible expresses the idea of "practices righteousness" best, it is translated "He who practices righteousness <who is upright, conforming to the divine will in purpose, thought, and action, living a consistently conscientious life> is righteous, even as He is righteous. In the translation of "practices sin"; it is translated "deliberately, knowingly, and habitually practices sin." Our Gracious Heavenly Father understands our frailty and though looking for ultimate perfection is looking for those whose pursuit is "seeking first the Kingdom of God".[45]

Staying in the book of 1 John chapter one verse 6 through chapter 2 verse 1, "If we say that we have fellowship with Him and *yet* walk in the darkness, we lie and do not practice the truth; but if we walk in the Light as He Himself is in the Light, we have fellowship with one another, and the blood of Jesus His Son cleanses us from all sin. If we say that we have no sin, we are deceiving ourselves and the truth is not in us. If we confess our sins, He is faithful and righteous to forgive us our sins and to cleanse us from all unrighteousness. If we say that we have not sinned, we make Him a liar and His word is not in us. My little children, I am writing these things to you so that you may not sin. And if anyone sins, we have an Advocate with the Father, Jesus Christ the righteous;"

Many testify of a relationship with Christ, they say with their words, "I believe in Jesus." This statement for them is their "bona fide" as if mere words constituted a vital connection with Christ. John throws a wet blanket over that mind set and snuffs out any sense of legitimacy it may hold. It is not words that justify for even the devils believe.[46] It is walking in the light. Jesus said, "I am the Light of the world; he who follows Me will not walk in the darkness, but will have the Light of life."[47]

Following Christ is the criteria used by God to determine our relation with the Light. To follow includes in its meaning, to join Him as His attendant and to accompany Him as one of His disciples. The result of following Jesus and walking in His light is, we have close communion and communication with the Light Himself. This fellowship/communion will naturally be reflected in our association and connection with fellow believers and those in the world.

There is an interesting phrase in 1 John one, "we have fellowship with one another, and the blood of Jesus His Son cleanses us from all sin". As we are walking in the Light where all things are open between us and the Lord, sins are quickly cleansed by His blood. The indication is, our very nearness to His wondrous light quickly reveals any wandering we may have and just as quickly, as we turn to Him, our sins are washed away. "But he who practices the truth comes to the Light, so that his deeds may be manifested as having been wrought in God."[48]

Let us now do away with one of the biggest issues faced by new and more mature Christians. None of us can claim we are without sin, it may be a sin of omission or commission, but we all must deal with sin. It is just a reality of our growing pains in the Lord. This being the case, can we simply accept that fact? If we can be honest and humble enough to see ourselves as we really are, then we will be able to quit fearing our sin and separation from God.

God, Who perfectly loves us and calls us His own child, does not want us to walk in condemnation and fear of judgment. His love dispels all fear and gives us the safety of choosing to be open about our sins and failures, for we have an Advocate with the Father. This reality does not give us license to participate in the works of darkness, but the beauteous liberty of instantly knowing we can be cleansed and forgiven by one who will not quickly throw us aside.

1Jo 4:18 There is no fear in love; but perfect love casts out fear, because fear involves punishment, and the one who fears is not perfected in love.

Ro 8:1 Therefore there is now no condemnation for those who are in Christ Jesus.

1 Jo 3;19,20 We will know by this that we are of the truth, and will assure our heart before Him in whatever our heart condemns us; for God is greater than our heart and knows all things.

ENGAGE IN THE BATTLE

Paul in his letter to the Corinthians described the warfare he was involved in as an apostle of the Lord Jesus. The issues were constantly before him while dealing with the immorality, idolatry and the wanton extravagance of the city Corinth. The pagan influence on the Corinthian church weighed heavy on his heart. Jealousy, division, false teachers, pride, misuse of the spiritual gifts, the Corinthian world view in many ways was the battle ground of the Church in Corinth. Paul in his letters with firm, intentional and yet loving words challenged the local Church to rid themselves of its worldly ways and to deal with and correct those issues.

Paul in his second letter to the Corinthian Church makes plain his battle plan in dealing with this wayward Church. "For though we walk in the flesh, we do not war according to the flesh, for the weapons of our warfare are not of the flesh, but divinely powerful for the destruction of fortresses. *We are* destroying speculations and every lofty thing raised up against the knowledge of God, and *we are* taking every thought captive to the obedience of Christ, and we are ready to punish all disobedience, whenever your obedience is complete."[49] Paul makes this statement in contrast to their outward and fleshly view and capitulation to the culture in which they were living. (Paul graciously enjoined the Church to come into complete obedience to the Gospel, thereby as a united community he could then properly bring discipline to those who were disobedient.)

Though these words were written by Paul to underline his dealings with the Corinthian Church, they are completely appropriate for us in dealing with our own flirtations with sin. We must in humility acknowledge that we are walking in our fleshly body with all its propensities and frailties, we have not arrived yet. As we read those verses, I find it instructive; there is no mention of things external. The warfare is all within, with ideas, concepts, and modes of thinking which contradict the true knowledge of God and His Kingdom. This war may not be won in a single skirmish, but it can be won, if we by the empowering of the Spirit of God bring truth to bear upon every inward thought and motivation. All that contradicts sound godly wisdom must be pulled down and made subject to Christ.[50]

There is no need for us to get involved in the fruitless definitions of what is sin and what is not sin, for we all know. Jesus briefly defines that which defiles a man in the book of Mark.

Jesus said, "That which proceeds out of the man, that is what defiles the man."For from within, out of the heart of men, proceed the evil thoughts, fornications, thefts, murders, adulteries, deeds of coveting *and* wickedness, *as well as* deceit, sensuality, envy, slander, pride *and* foolishness. "All these evil things proceed from within and defile the man."[51]

Paul also speaks to those things which proceed from our fleshly nature. "Now the deeds of the flesh are evident, which are: immorality, impurity, sensuality, idolatry, sorcery, enmities, strife, jealousy, outbursts of anger, disputes, dissensions, factions, envying, drunkenness, carousing, and things like these, of which I forewarn you, just as I have forewarned you, that those who practice such things will not inherit the kingdom of God."[52]

Therefore, let us take full responsibility for our actions and the consequences of those actions before Him with Whom we have to do. And lastly, in dealing with the cultivation of our **garden** let's give heed to the admonition of Paul and **run to win**.

1 Corinthians 9: 24-27 "Do you not know that those who run in a race all run, but *only* one receives the prize? Run in such a way that you may win. Everyone who competes in the games exercises self-control in all things. They then *do it* to receive a perishable wreath, but we an imperishable. Therefore I run in such a way, as not without aim; I box in such a way, as not beating the air; but I discipline my body and make it my slave, so that, after I have preached to others, I myself will not be disqualified"

Here are a few good ways to cultivate your heart garden.

Keep a short account before God. Quickly handle sin or any sense of separation from Him.

Keep short accounts with those around you; be quick to forgive and to ask forgiveness.

Pray in the Spirit often.[53]

Read and Study the Sermon on the Mount.   Matthew chapter 5,6,7

Read and reread the Gospels.

In the Old Testament, note the "ways" of God in His dealings with men and nations.

Check out the other New Testament commands. These are a good litmus test for your walk.

Use a concordance find and apply the "one anothers" in the Scriptures.

Make the Psalms and Proverbs a regular part of your devotions.

Review 1 Corinthians 13 occasionally, the chapter on Love.

Cultivate a quiet and open heart before the Lord; in silence learn to be in His presence.

Develop your individual method of devotions & study. Adapt or change as you grow.

Philippians 4:8 Finally, brethren, whatever is true, whatever is honorable, whatever is right, whatever is pure, whatever is lovely, whatever is of good repute, if there is any excellence and if anything worthy of praise, dwell on these things.

DEALING WITH DEMONIC OPPRESSION

Before we get too deep in our discussion, I would like to make a few observations. First, "You cannot cast out the flesh or the "old nature" nor can you crucify an evil spirit. Each must be dealt with in a scriptural manner." The flesh, our old nature, has been crucified with Christ.[54]

Secondly, in the New American Standard Bible there are two words in Scripture which are related to the subject of "dealing with the devil", "oppressed" and "possessed". When the Scripture uses the word oppressed and its variants, it means to tire down with toil, exhaust with labor, to afflict or oppress with evils, to make trouble for, to treat roughly. It can also mean, to bruise, to break, break in pieces, shatter, smite through, and to exercise harsh control over one, to use one's power against one. The second word, possessed, as used in Scripture is translated demon possessed. The meaning is, "to be under the power or control of a demon". These two words must be understood in the context in which they are used. (Information gathered from Strong's Concordance)

The devil and his cohorts do not play fair. Through the use of guile, deception, whispered lies, and even traumatic experiences, they look for a position of leverage in order to take advantage of individuals. In response to this barrage of deception there are choices we can make. We can submit to God and resist the evil or we can fall under their trickery.[55] Please note how the teachings of Christ and the Apostles enable us to guard our hearts from the enemy's deceit.

Fortunately, "… if we walk in the Light as He Himself is in the Light, we have fellowship with one another, and the blood of Jesus His Son cleanses us from all sin."[56] Most often though we will find, as Christians, long before our enemy can gain a foothold in our lives the Spirit of Christ within has begun to change our old ways and manner of thinking. God in His wonderful love and abundant grace truly is our shield and our high tower.[57] Even as new believers, God in His infinite love and unimaginable grace will protect and guard your heart and soul as you continue to follow hard after Him. "Be anxious for nothing, but in everything by prayer and supplication with thanksgiving let your requests be made known to God. And the peace of God, which surpasses all comprehension, will guard your hearts and your minds in Christ Jesus."[58]

Develop your walk with the Christ in submission to the Spirit's promptings and in pursuit of the Kingdom of God and you will find attacks by the enemy, whether frequent or often, will cause you to grow more and more victorious. "… but thanks be to God, who gives us the victory through our Lord Jesus Christ."[59] "For whatever is born of God overcomes the world; and this is the victory that has overcome the world our faith."[60]

2 Thessalonians 3:3 "But the Lord is faithful, and He will strengthen and protect you from the evil one."

Those that have believed in and trusted in Christ as their Savior have been taken out of kingdom of darkness and brought in to the Kingdom of Light. The need for deliverance from demonic possession if necessary occurs prior to entrance to God's Kingdom. After entrance into the Kingdom, the enemy can only gain access to oppress us if we come into agreement with his deception. An example of this might be, to choose not to forgive someone who has wronged us. This action or inaction can allow the enemy to oppress and torment us, while at the same time the Holy Spirit is trying to convict us and draw us back in relationship to the Father. Another example men and women are facing especially in our current liberal culture is the area of lust and immoral behavior in its various forms. As in the letter written by James, the devil doesn't make us do it; we are tempted when drawn away by our own choice, our own lust.[61] And true to the principle of choice, with each choice we make we must deal with the consequences which come as a result of those choices.

The results of spirit oppression may have the effect of tremendous agitation, fear, and a sense of being out of control. But the individual under attack can readily seek and gain freedom in the area of oppression by repentance and choosing the reign of Christ in the affected area of their lives. This may include the assistance of a fellow believer who may be gifted in the area of discernment, the word of knowledge and who also moves with spiritual authority.

A quick word about physical and mental trauma, either of these can bring a period depression and anxiety. This is not imaginary; it is a real phenomenon which may be handled in a number of ways. The emotional impact of a trauma may be enormous, requiring significant help from professionals. If there is a physical deficiency that can be met medically, there is nothing wrong with that form of intervention. In that situation one should continue to seek the Lord for healing.

At the risk of seeming unsympathetic and callous with reference to emotional or mental trauma, the cure is often to come into acceptance of the event or experience, avoiding any denial. Then making a choice to either forgive or to no longer allow the chains of the experience to keep us bound to the past. Inner healing with the aid of someone mature in Christ can be a marvelous answer for many. Regardless, all who experience these depths of trauma must guard their hearts and minds for as stated before, the enemy does not play fair. If he can he will try to gain access and bring a spirit of oppression to bear and exacerbate the problem. Even in these areas one need not accept defeat for we are more than overcomers.

1John 4:4 You are from God, little children, and have overcome them; because greater is He who is in you than he who is in the world.

1John 5:4, 5 "For whatever is born of God overcomes the world; and this is the victory that has overcome the world our faith. Who is the one who overcomes the world, but he who believes that Jesus is the Son of God?"

I will try to paint a simplistic picture of the way our enemy gains access in order to oppress us. Picture your soul life which consists of your mind, will, and emotions as a "soul pie". This "soul pie" is the area within us which is being transformed into the image of Christ. The Holy Spirit Who dwells in the once dead spirit of each believer is constantly working to bring every area of our "soul pie" into the obedience of Christ.[62] Each slice of the "soul pie" represents an area in our lives in which we have the right to choose who will reign in that area.

Let us choose the area of money, the question becomes, "Do I solely determine where and how I will spend or give my money or will the Lord guide me in those decisions?" If I am a covetous person or I am miserly and stingy then this slice of my "soul pie" is an area in my life where the Holy Spirit can, as of yet, not inhabit. The end result may be that the enemy could bring oppression into my life because of the sin I have in covetousness and the love of money. The enemy can use this slice of my "soul pie" to influence other areas in my life and disrupt my fellowship with the Lord and with God's kids. This influence may be only a slight irritant or it may become a very serious road block to the work of God in our lives, in either case it should be dealt with as soon as it is recognized.

The resolution may be as simple as repentance and bringing our use of money in submission to the Lord. Or, it may require the insight of those that walk in maturity with us and can enable us to bring the affected area into the light of Christ. Once it is exposed, through repentance and in authority, we can command the enemy to take his oppressive work in the area which has affected us and to leave. His access to our lives in that area is no longer available; he has been "cast off".

Another picture might be that of a leech or a tick, which secretly attaches itself to our body and begins to drain our life blood. Amazingly, many times we are not immediately aware of the infestation until it has become quite gorged with our blood. There may even be the need for someone else to discover the foreign attacker and we might need their help in removing it.[63] Once it has been removed the immediate affected area must be cleansed and begin the healing process. In a sense we have "cast off" the enemy of our body which was sucking our very life forces from us.

Sometimes, life's circumstances can be the crucible which is our challenge. Accidents, deaths, even the choices of others may impact our lives. How we handle them will be the measure of our dependence upon God. Does it knock us off our feet? If it does, how quickly do we get up. Do we forgive? Do we blame? Do we desire revenge? Do we fall into our own personal pity party? Has God somehow suddenly abandoned us? The question really becomes, who moved, me or God?

"Beloved, I urge you as aliens and strangers to abstain from fleshly lusts which wage war against the soul." (1 Pe 2:11)

"Beloved, I pray that in all respects you may prosper and be in good health, just as your soul prospers." (3Jo 1:2)

"By your steadfastness *and* patient endurance you shall win the true life of your souls." (Lu 21:19 Amplified Bible)

DEALING WITH A FRONTAL ATTACK OF THE ENEMY

Dealing with overt attacks of the enemy may be much easier to recognize than to deal with, than those which directly appeal to our inner soulish nature. These attacks may come in many forms, all of which demand that one be diligent and discerning. The enemy may use a person or a particular situation to bring to bear his deceitful tactic. Refusing to take the bait may well be the best defense in that circumstance. Note how Jesus handled the visceral hatred and slander and physical attacks the enemy was able to instigate within those around Him. No wonder in the end He could pray, "Father, forgive them; for they do not know what they are doing."[64]

On occasion, your adversary may come against you and you will be aware of a sense of deep darkness or evil. The resultant fear or confusion should prompt you to immediately stand firm in faith and exercise the authority you have in the name of Jesus. Demand, don't ask, demand the darkness to be gone in the name of the Lord Jesus Christ. "Submit therefore to God. Resist the devil and he will flee from you."[65]

I am reminded of a story that I heard many years ago. A young man was late for work and rushed to the bus stop to catch a ride downtown. He arrived in time at the stop but happened to notice his dog had followed him from home. Not willing to make a scene he told the dog to go home and pointed in that direction. After several attempts trying to get the dog to head back home and noticing the bus was nearly at his bus stop, the young man stomped his feet, ran toward the dog and yelled for it to go home right now. The dog with its tail between its legs took off and made it home just as the bus pulled up. The moral is sometimes we need to mean business when confronting our adversary.

LASTLY

By now you have noticed the predominance of this study has to do with our inward walk with God. The reason must be obvious, if we keep our relationship with the Lord on a good foundation, most of the battles we face will be in the arena of self. I can speak authoritatively about this because for over 50 years I have found my greatest problems were not those outside of me. My greatest difficulty was me. This allowed me to put "spiritual warfare" in its proper place in my life. When faced with an issue, I must first look at my own heart. Does my heart and my response reflect the new life I have in Christ? What does the Lord want to teach me in what I am now facing?

War has been declared but, "But in all these things we overwhelmingly conquer through Him who loved us."[66]

As we bring this study to a close, I realize there may be many loose ends and unanswered questions that you may have, but remember you are not alone. "... for He Himself has said, "I WILL NEVER DESERT YOU, NOR WILL I EVER FORSAKE YOU,"[67] Everything you face, every situation that confronts you, each person who may hurt or defame you, all which comes your way must be filtered through the hand and will of God. And, "No temptation has overtaken you but such as is common to man; and God is faithful, who will not allow you to be tempted beyond what you are able, but with the temptation will provide the way of escape also, so that you will be able to endure it." [68]God in His wisdom will use each thing that touches our lives to teach us our utter dependence upon Him as our source and strength.

"Beloved, do not believe every spirit, but test the spirits to see whether they are from God, because many false prophets have gone out into the world. By this you know the Spirit of God: every spirit that confesses that Jesus Christ has come in the flesh is from God; and every spirit that does not confess Jesus is not from God; this is the *spirit* of the antichrist, of which you have heard that it is coming, and now it is already in the world. You are from God, little children, and have overcome them; because greater is He who is in you than he who is in the world."[69]

"Now may the God of peace Himself sanctify you entirely; and may your spirit and soul and body be preserved complete, without blame at the coming of our Lord Jesus Christ."[70]

---

[1] Is 14:12-14 "How you have fallen from heaven, O star of the morning, son of the dawn! You have been cut down to the earth, You who have weakened the nations! "But you said in your heart, 'I will ascend to heaven; I will raise my throne above the stars of God, And I will sit on the mount of assembly In the recesses of the north. 'I will ascend above the heights of the clouds; I will make myself like the Most High.'

[2] Eph 2:1,2 1 ¶ And you were dead in your trespasses and sins, in which you formerly walked according to the course of this world, according to the prince of the power of the air, of the spirit that is now working in the sons of disobedience.

[3] Gen 1:26 Then God said, "Let Us make man in Our image, according to Our likeness; and let them rule over the fish of the sea and over the birds of the sky and over the cattle and over all the earth, and over every creeping thing that creeps on the earth."

[4] Gen 2:16,17 The LORD God commanded the man, saying, "From any tree of the garden you may eat freely; but from the tree of the knowledge of good and evil you shall not eat, for in the day that you eat from it you will surely die."

[5] Mt 6:24 "No one can serve two masters; for either he will hate the one and love the other, or he will be devoted to one and despise the other. You cannot serve God and wealth."

[6] Rom 6:16 Do you not know that when you present yourselves to someone *as* slaves for obedience, you are slaves of the one whom you obey, either of sin resulting in death, or of obedience resulting in righteousness?

[7] Mt 5:21,27,33,38,43 "You have heard ..., but I say to you..."

[8] Heb 1:1-3 God, after He spoke long ago to the fathers in the prophets in many portions and in many ways, in these last days has spoken to us in His Son, whom He appointed heir of all things, through whom also He made the world. And

He is the radiance of His glory and the exact representation of His nature, and upholds all things by the word of His power. When He had made purification of sins, He sat down at the right hand of the Majesty on high,

[9] Joh 14:9

[10] Mt 6:9

[11] Jo 16:23

[12] Jo 3:16 "For God so loved the world, that He gave His only begotten Son, that whoever believes in Him shall not perish, but have eternal life.

[13] Ez 20:44 "Therefore say to the house of Israel, 'Thus says the Lord GOD, "It is not for your sake, O house of Israel, that I am about to act, but for My holy name, which you have profaned among the nations where you went.

Ez 36:22, 23 "I will vindicate the holiness of My great name which has been profaned among the nations, which you have profaned in their midst. Then the nations will know that I am the LORD," declares the Lord GOD, "when I prove My-self holy among you in their sight."Then you will know that I am the LORD when I have dealt with you for My name's sake, not according to your evil ways or according to your corrupt deeds, O house of Israel," declares the Lord GOD.'"

[14] 1 Jo 2:12 I am writing to you, little children, because your sins have been forgiven you for His name's sake.

[15] Gen 1:26, 27 Then God said, "Let Us make man in Our image, according to Our likeness; and let them rule over the fish of the sea and over the birds of the sky and over the cattle and over all the earth, and over every creeping thing that creeps on the earth." God created man in His own image, in the image of God He created him; male and female He created them.

[16] Jn 1: 1 In the beginning was the Word, and the Word was with God, and the Word was God.

Jn 1: 14 And the Word became flesh, and dwelt among us, and we saw His glory, glory as of the only begotten from the Father, full of grace and truth.

Ga 4:4 But when the fullness of the time came, God sent forth His Son, born of a woman, born under the Law,

[17] Rom 8:29 For those whom He foreknew, He also predestined *to become* conformed to the image of His Son, so that He would be the firstborn among many brethren;

[18] Gen 2:18 Then the LORD God said, "It is not good for the man to be alone; I will make him a helper suitable for him."

[19] Gen 2:20 The man gave names to all the cattle, and to the birds of the sky, and to every beast of the field, but for Adam there was not found a helper suitable for him.

[20] Col 3:10 and have put on the new self who is being renewed to a true knowledge according to the image of the One who created him

2 Cor 3:18 But we all, with unveiled face, beholding as in a mirror the glory of the Lord, are being transformed into the same image from glory to glory,

just as from the Lord, the Spirit.

[21] Rev 2:10 'Do not fear what you are about to suffer. Behold, the devil is about to cast some of you into prison, so that you will be tested, and you will have tribulation for ten days. Be faithful until death, and I will give you the crown of life.

Rev 2:17 'He who has an ear, let him hear what the Spirit says to the churches. To him who overcomes, to him I will give *some* of the hidden manna, and I will give him a white stone, and a new name written on the stone which no one knows but he who receives it.'

[22] Gen 2:16,17 The LORD God commanded the man, saying, "From any tree of the garden you may eat freely; but from the tree of the knowledge of good and evil you shall not eat, for in the day that you eat from it you will surely die." *(Also note, it is the knowledge of "good" and "evil")*

[23] Gen 3:8 They heard the sound of the LORD God walking in the garden in the cool of the day, and the man and his wife hid themselves from the presence of the LORD God among the trees of the garden.

[24] Rom 5:16-18 The gift is not like *that which came* through the one who sinned; for on the one hand the judgment *arose* from one *transgression* resulting in condemnation, but on the other hand the free gift *arose* from many transgressions resulting in justification. For if by the transgression of the one, death reigned through the one, much more those who receive the abundance of grace and of the gift of righteousness will reign in life through the One, Jesus Christ. So then as through one transgression there resulted condemnation to all men, even so through one act of righteousness there resulted justification of life to all men.

[25] Rom 8:19-22 For the anxious longing of the creation waits eagerly for the revealing of the sons of God. For the creation was subjected to futility, not willingly, but because of Him who subjected it, in hope that the creation itself also will be set free from its slavery to corruption into the freedom of the glory of the children of God. For we know that the whole creation groans and suffers the pains of childbirth together until now.

[26] Mrk 12:29-31 Jesus answered, "The foremost is, 'HEAR, O ISRAEL! THE LORD OUR GOD IS ONE LORD; AND YOU SHALL LOVE THE LORD YOUR GOD WITH ALL YOUR HEART, AND WITH ALL YOUR SOUL, AND WITH ALL YOUR MIND, AND WITH ALL YOUR STRENGTH.' "The second is this, 'YOU SHALL LOVE YOUR NEIGHBOR AS YOURSELF.' There is no other commandment greater than these."

[27] Eph 2:8,9 For by grace you have been saved through faith; and that not of yourselves, it is the gift of God; not as a result of works, so that no one may boast.

Rom 12:33 For through the grace given to me I say to everyone among you not to think more highly of himself than he ought to think; but to think so as to have sound judgment, as God has allotted to each a measure of faith.

[28] Heb 12:4-11 You have not yet resisted to the point of shedding blood in your striving against sin; and you have forgotten the exhortation which is addressed

to you as sons, "MY SON, DO NOT REGARD LIGHTLY THE DISCIPLINE OF THE LORD, NOR FAINT WHEN YOU ARE REPROVED BY HIM; FOR THOSE WHOM THE LORD LOVES HE DISCIPLINES, AND HE SCOURGES EVERY SON WHOM HE RECEIVES." It is for discipline that you endure; God deals with you as with sons; for what son is there whom *his* father does not discipline? But if you are without discipline, of which all have become partakers, then you are illegitimate children and not sons. Furthermore, we had earthly fathers to discipline us, and we respected them; shall we not much rather be subject to the Father of spirits, and live? For they disciplined us for a short time as seemed best to them, but He *disciplines us* for *our* good, so that we may share His holiness.

[29] Rom 8:10 If Christ is in you, though the body is dead because of sin, yet the spirit is alive because of righteousness.

[30] Eph 3:16 that He would grant you, according to the riches of His glory, to be strengthened with power through His Spirit in the inner man,

Eph 3: 20 Now to Him who is able to do far more abundantly beyond all that we ask or think, according to the power that works within us,   (Also read Romans 6:3-ff)

[31]Phil 1:11 having been filled with the fruit of righteousness which *comes* through Jesus Christ, to the glory and praise of God.

[32] Jam 5:16 Therefore, confess your sins to one another, and pray for one another so that you may be healed. The effective prayer of a righteous man can accomplish much.

1 Cor 6:12 All things are lawful for me, but not all things are profitable. All things are lawful for me, but I will not be mastered by anything.

1 Cor 10: 23 All things are lawful, but not all things are profitable. All things are lawful, but not all things edify.

[33] Ex 23:22 "But if you truly obey his voice and do all that I say, then I will be an enemy to your enemies and an adversary to your adversaries.

[34] Ex 23:29,30

[35] Eph 5: 10 trying to learn what is pleasing to the Lord.

[36] 1 Cor 1:26-29

[37] Phil 4:13; Gal 2:20

[38] Rom 6:3-7

[39] 2 Pet 3:15, 16 and regard the patience of our Lord *as* salvation; just as also our beloved brother Paul, according to the wisdom given him, wrote to you, as also in all *his* letters, speaking in them of these things, in which are some things hard to understand, which the untaught and unstable distort, as *they do* also the rest of the Scriptures, to their own destruction.

[40] 1 Cor 12:13 For by one Spirit we were all baptized into one body, whether Jews or Greeks, whether slaves or free, and we were all made to drink of one Spirit.

[41] Rom 6: 4 Therefore we have been buried with Him through baptism into

death, so that as Christ was raised from the dead through the glory of the Father, so we too might walk in newness of life.

[42] Rom 8:14 For all who are being led by the Spirit of God, these are sons of God.

[43] Romans 7:5 For while we were in the flesh, the sinful passions, which were *aroused* by the Law, were at work in the members of our body to bear fruit for death.

Romans 8:2 For the law of the Spirit of life in Christ Jesus has set you free from the law of sin and of death.

1 Corinthians 15:56 The sting of death is sin, and the power of sin is the law;

[44] Jam 1:13-15 Let no one say when he is tempted, "I am being tempted by God"; for God cannot be tempted by evil, and He Himself does not tempt anyone. But each one is tempted when he is carried away and enticed by his own lust. Then when lust has conceived, it gives birth to sin; and when sin is accomplished, it brings forth death.

[45] Mt 5:48 "Therefore you are to be perfect, as your heavenly Father is perfect."

Mt 6:33 "But seek first His kingdom and His righteousness, and all these things will be added to you."

[46] Jam 2:19 You believe that God is one. You do well; the demons also believe, and shudder.

[47] John 8:12

[48] John 3:21

[49] 2 Cor 10:3-6

[50] Heb 12:9 Furthermore, we had earthly fathers to discipline us, and we respected them; shall we not much rather be subject to the Father of spirits, and live?

Gal 5:1 It was for freedom that Christ set us free; therefore keep standing firm and do not be **subject** again to a yoke of slavery.

[51] Mk 7:20-23

[52] Gal 5:19-21

[53] Jude 1:20 But you, beloved, building yourselves up on your most holy faith, praying in the Holy Spirit

[54] Rom 6:5-7 For if we have become united with Him in the likeness of His death, certainly we shall also be *in the likeness* of His resurrection, knowing this, that our old self was crucified with Him, in order that our body of sin might be done away with, so that we would no longer be slaves to sin; for he who has died is freed from sin.

Gal 2:20 "I have been crucified with Christ; and it is no longer I who live, but Christ lives in me; and the *life* which I now live in the flesh I live by faith in the Son of God, who loved me and gave Himself up for me.

Gal 5:24 Now those who belong to Christ Jesus have crucified the flesh with its passions and desires.

[55] Jam 4:7 Submit therefore to God. Resist the devil and he will flee from you.

[56] 1 John 1:7

[57] Ps 3: 3 But You, O LORD, are a shield about me, My glory, and the One who lifts my head.

Ps 18: 2 The LORD is my rock and my fortress and my deliverer, My God, my rock, in whom I take refuge; My shield and the horn of my salvation, my stronghold.

Prov 18:10 The name of the LORD is a strong tower; The righteous runs into it and is safe.

[58] Phil 4:6,7

[59] 1 Cor 15:57

[60] 1 Jo 5:4

[61] Jam 1: 13-15 Let no one say when he is tempted, "I am being tempted by God"; for God cannot be tempted by evil, and He Himself does not tempt anyone. But each one is tempted when he is carried away and enticed by his own lust. Then when lust has conceived, it gives birth to sin; and when sin is accomplished, it brings forth death.

[62] 2 Cor 10:5 We are destroying speculations and every lofty thing raised up against the knowledge of God, and *we are* taking every thought captive to the obedience of Christ,

[63] Jam 5: 16 Therefore, confess your sins to one another, and pray for one another so that you may be healed. The effective prayer of a righteous man can accomplish much.

[64] Luke 23:34

[65] James 4:7

[66] Romans 8:37

[67] Hebrews 13:5b

[68] 1Co 10:13 No temptation has overtaken you but such as is common to man; and God is faithful, who will not allow you to be tempted beyond what you are able, but with the temptation will provide the way of escape also, so that you will be able to endure it.

[69] 1 John 4:1-4

[70] 1 Thessalonians 5:23

When one speaks of spiritual warfare, one conjures up images of late-night horror movies and black clothed clergy speaking in hushed tones. A room filled with dim lights and secret incantations. Misunderstanding and fear abound when it comes to this subject. For the most part, it is thought to be a subject best left to the professioanals. Besides, you don't want to make the devil mad.

The truth is that he is mad already and has been since his ouster from the heavenly realms. One of his goals is to keep each of us in the dark about the battle we face and in the dark about his existence. One of his ploys is to make light of the issue. He probably instigated the phrase we all have heard used, "the devil made me do it."

His other goal is to deny his impact upon our lives and the ways that he uses life experiences and circumstances to gain access to those who are believers in Christ. Difficulties with personal relationships, environmental problems, medical issues, life in general are all fair game for him to play on our doubts, fears and emotions. War has been declared and we can choose on which side we are going to be.

Buckle up, you are in control, if you are a twice born Christian. Your strength comes from He who dwells in eternal glorious light. His name is the Lord Jesus Christ. He has already defeated your enemy and has risen as a conqueror to sit at the right hand of God Almighty.

Your part in the battle is, with faith in His victory, to face it head on and choose His ways and not your own. You can and must take control, with God's help, of your inward self. Your mind, will, and emotions are where the devil wants you to do battle. If he can keep you in the realm of your self-life, he will defeat you every time.

Ours is to not meet him in our own strength, but in the power

that comes from choosing to respond from our relationship with the Lord. If someone has wronged us, we forgive. If life goes south on us, we draw from His strength and endure. If we are sad or depressed, we draw upon strength from His word and prayer. We learn, we are not alone, we are a part of His body.

Made in the USA
Columbia, SC
07 June 2020